ALL ABOUT

NORTHERN IRELAND

BY SUSAN HARRISON

BookLife
PUBLISHING

©2020
BookLife Publishing Ltd.
King's Lynn
Norfolk PE30 4LS

ISBN: 978-1-83927-113-7

All rights reserved
Printed in Malaysia

A catalogue record for this book
is available from the British Library.

Written by:
Susan Harrison

Edited by:
Joanna Brundle

Designed by:
Drue Rintoul

CONTENTS

Words that look like **this** can be found in the glossary on page 30.

WELCOME TO NORTHERN IRELAND

Area:
Around 14,000 square kilometres (km)

Currency:
British Pounds (£)

Official Language:
English & Irish Gaelic

SCOTLAND

NORTHERN IRELAND

Population:
1,800,000

IRELAND

Capital City:
Belfast

WALES

ENGLAND

Northern Ireland is one of four countries which, together with **England, Wales** and **Scotland,** form the **United Kingdom.**

Northern Ireland is part of an island, and is bordered by the Republic of Ireland. Most of the people on the island live in the Republic of Ireland.

TAKE A LOOK **www.discovernorthernireland.com** is a great place to look for information about Northern Ireland.

Northern Ireland is famous for its glacial valleys and mountains, lush countryside, Norman castles and its many golf courses.

IN 1800, BEFORE THE INTRODUCTION OF GAS STREET LIGHTS, ANYONE CAUGHT PUTTING OUT A STREET LIGHT IN BELFAST COULD BE PUT IN PRISON FOR SIX MONTHS!

THE GIANT'S CAUSEWAY IS ONE OF THE MOST FAMOUS <u>LANDMARKS</u> IN NORTHERN IRELAND.

THE HISTORY OF NORTHERN IRELAND

It is believed that people arrived in Ireland around 500 <u>BC</u>. Their <u>culture</u>, religion and history can still be seen around the whole country. Christianity was introduced to the country by St Patrick who arrived in Saul in County Down in 432.

Northern Ireland was created after the **partition** of Ireland in 1921, when the six counties of Ulster became part of the United Kingdom.

THERE ARE MANY REMINDERS OF EARLY HISTORY IN NORTHERN IRELAND, INCLUDING CROSSES SUCH AS THIS ONE.

THE NORTHERN IRELAND ASSEMBLY IS BASED AT STORMONT. THE PEOPLE WHO WORK HERE ARE RESPONSIBLE FOR MAKING LAWS FOR NORTHERN IRELAND.

500 BC – People arrive in Ireland

1171 – The Irish kings knelt before Henry II of England and called him the High King

1650 – Oliver Cromwell tries to assert English control in Ireland

1801 – The Act of Union unites Ireland and Britain

432 – St Patrick arrives in Ireland and introduces Christianity

1558–1603 – Elizabeth I rules Ireland

1690 – Battle of the Boyne, Protestant King William of Orange (William III) fights Roman Catholic King James II to keep Protestant and English rule in Ireland

TAKE A LOOK For lots of information about the history of Northern Ireland, have a look online at **www.askaboutireland.ie**

THE OLD BELFAST CASTLE WAS BUILT IN THE 1170s BY JOHN DE COURCY. THE CURRENT BELFAST CASTLE WASN'T BUILT UNTIL THE 1870s.

MANY PEOPLE WERE KILLED DURING THE TROUBLES.

The period of time known as The Troubles during the 1970s and 1980s saw **conflict** between different groups in Northern Ireland and the UK government.

ST PATRICK'S CHURCH IN ARMAGH WAS FOUNDED BY ST PATRICK WHEN HE INTRODUCED CHRISTIANITY TO IRELAND.

1916 – The Easter Rising – The Irish Republican Brotherhood seize government buildings in Dublin

1921 – Partition. Six counties become Northern Ireland

1998 – The Belfast Agreement is signed, and the Northern Ireland Assembly is elected

1846–1852 The Great Irish Famine

1919 – A new Irish government is set up and they say they will be independent from the UK

1969 – The start of The Troubles which last around 30 years

LANDMARKS

Northern Ireland is full of famous landmarks which attract millions of visitors every year. They help to tell the story of the history of the country as well as shaping the <u>landscape</u>.

Some of them, such as Mussenden Temple, the **political murals** in Belfast and the many castles and memorials around the country, are made by humans.

THE BALLYCOPELAND WINDMILL WAS BUILT IN THE LATE 1700s. IT WAS REPAIRED IN THE LATE 1900s AND IS NOW NORTHERN IRELAND'S ONLY WORKING HISTORIC WINDMILL.

ST ANNE'S CATHEDRAL IN BELFAST IS ALSO KNOWN AS BELFAST CATHEDRAL. THE FOUNDATION STONE WAS LAID IN 1899.

THE GIANT'S RING IN BALLYNAHATTY NEAR BELFAST IS 180 METRES (M) IN <u>DIAMETER</u> WITH A STONE TOMB IN THE MIDDLE. IT IS THOUGHT TO BE MORE THAN 4,000 YEARS OLD.

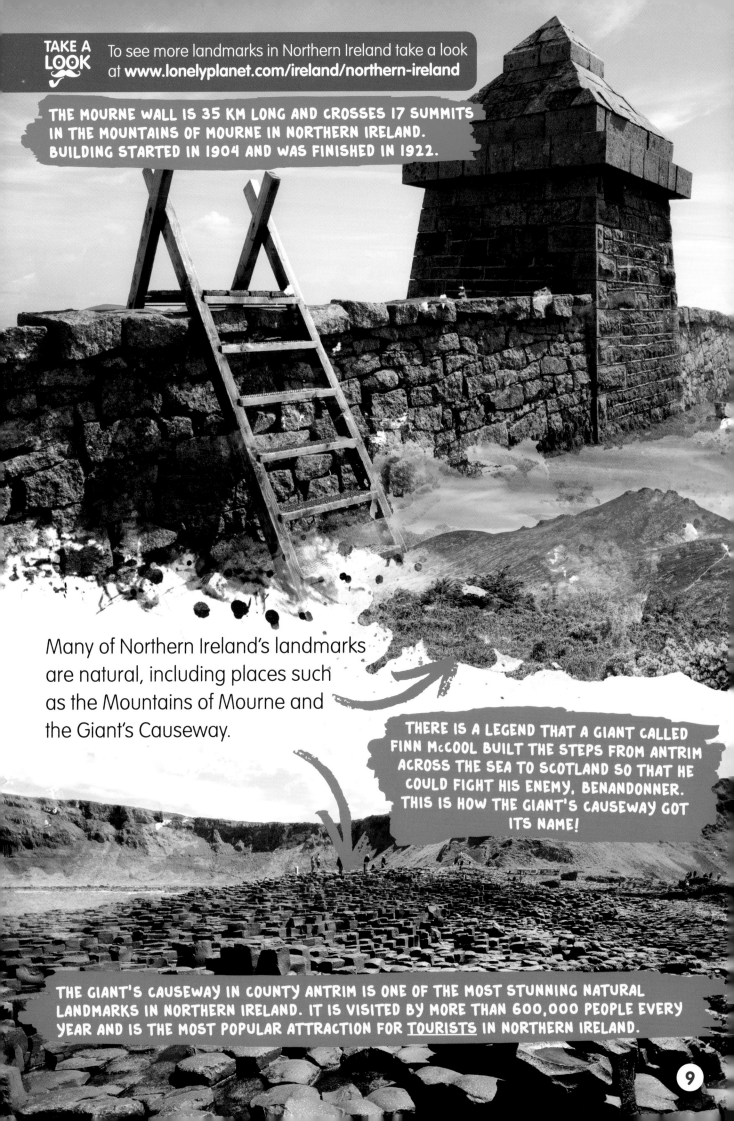

TAKE A LOOK To see more landmarks in Northern Ireland take a look at www.lonelyplanet.com/ireland/northern-ireland

THE MOURNE WALL IS 35 KM LONG AND CROSSES 17 SUMMITS IN THE MOUNTAINS OF MOURNE IN NORTHERN IRELAND. BUILDING STARTED IN 1904 AND WAS FINISHED IN 1922.

Many of Northern Ireland's landmarks are natural, including places such as the Mountains of Mourne and the Giant's Causeway.

THERE IS A LEGEND THAT A GIANT CALLED FINN McCOOL BUILT THE STEPS FROM ANTRIM ACROSS THE SEA TO SCOTLAND SO THAT HE COULD FIGHT HIS ENEMY, BENANDONNER. THIS IS HOW THE GIANT'S CAUSEWAY GOT ITS NAME!

THE GIANT'S CAUSEWAY IN COUNTY ANTRIM IS ONE OF THE MOST STUNNING NATURAL LANDMARKS IN NORTHERN IRELAND. IT IS VISITED BY MORE THAN 600,000 PEOPLE EVERY YEAR AND IS THE MOST POPULAR ATTRACTION FOR <u>TOURISTS</u> IN NORTHERN IRELAND.

CLIMATE & LANDSCAPE

The <u>climate</u> of Northern Ireland is often mild, moist and changeable. There is plenty of rainfall, and it has cool summers and mild winters.

The landscape of Northern Ireland varies greatly. There are rolling hills and mountains, rivers and waterfalls. There is also farmland, coastlines and saltwater lakes.

THE GLENARIFF FOREST PARK HAS FOREST TRAILS, RIVERSIDE WALKS AND WATERFALLS.

MANY PARTS OF NORTHERN IRELAND ARE LUSH AND GREEN THANKS TO THE MILD, MOIST AND CHANGEABLE CLIMATE.

TAKE A LOOK For information about some of the lovely landscapes to visit, look at **www.discovernorthernireland.com**

THE NORTH ANTRIM COAST IS JUST ONE OF THE SPECTACULAR, VARIED LANDSCAPES OF NORTHERN IRELAND.

There are many nature reserves in Northern Ireland, which protect and promote the natural landscape of the country.

SLIEVE DONARD IN THE MOURNE MOUNTAINS IS THE HIGHEST PEAK IN NORTHERN IRELAND.

THE SPERRIN MOUNTAINS ARE ONE OF THE LARGEST UPLAND AREAS IN THE WHOLE OF IRELAND. MANY OF THEIR SLOPES ARE COVERED IN HEATHER.

TOWNS & CITIES

Most people in Northern Ireland live in towns and cities.

Over a million people live in counties Antrim and Down alone. Belfast is the largest city in Northern Ireland, and has a population of over 340,000. It is the 17th-largest city in the whole of the United Kingdom.

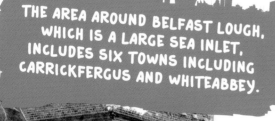

THE AREA AROUND BELFAST LOUGH, WHICH IS A LARGE SEA INLET, INCLUDES SIX TOWNS INCLUDING CARRICKFERGUS AND WHITEABBEY.

ARMAGH CITY IS HOME TO THE ARMAGH OBSERVATORY WHICH WAS BUILT IN 1790. IT IS A VERY IMPORTANT <u>RESEARCH FACILITY</u> FOR ASTRONOMERS.

WOMEN COULD WORK OR STUDY AT QUEEN'S UNIVERSITY IN THE CITY OF BELFAST 12 YEARS BEFORE THEY WERE ALLOWED TO STUDY AT OXFORD IN ENGLAND.

LONDONDERRY (DERRY) WAS ONE OF THE CITIES IN NORTHERN IRELAND SERIOUSLY AFFECTED BY THE TROUBLES. THERE ARE MANY MURALS AROUND THE CITY <u>DEPICTING</u> THOSE TIMES.

Towns and cities are important areas for healthcare, schools, colleges, shopping and sports facilities.

BELFAST CONTAINS OVER 12,000 SQUARE KM OF PARKLAND.

THE PEACE BRIDGE IN LONDONDERRY WAS OPENED IN 2011. IT IS A CYCLE PATH AND FOOTBRIDGE ACROSS THE RIVER FOYLE.

THE COUNTRYSIDE & WILDLIFE

The countryside of Northern Ireland is full of natural beauty, with a patchwork of fields, rolling hills, woodlands, mountains and lakes.

Around one-third of the population of Northern Ireland lives in the countryside and rural areas. Many of these people work on farms. Crops range from cereals, such as wheat and barley, to potatoes and fruit crops. There are also many farms that work with livestock such as sheep, cows and chickens.

THE NORTHERN LAPWING MAKES ITS HOME IN IRELAND.

THERE ARE AROUND 24,000 FARMS IN NORTHERN IRELAND.

THE FROTHY FLOWERS OF COWBANE CAN BE FOUND IN MARSHES AND DITCHES, AND ARE MORE COMMON IN NORTHERN IRELAND THAN ANY OTHER PART OF THE UK.

THE RED KITE AND THE PEREGRINE FALCON ARE INCREASING IN NUMBERS IN NORTHERN IRELAND.

There are many species of wildlife in the countryside of Northern Ireland which are protected by nature reserves.

COMMON SEALS CAN OFTEN BE SPOTTED IN AND AROUND STRANGFORD LOUGH, WHICH IS ONE OF THE MOST IMPORTANT BREEDING SITES FOR THE SPECIES IN NORTHERN IRELAND.

BADGERS, FOXES, DEER AND RABBITS CAN BE SEEN ALL OVER THE NORTHERN IRISH COUNTRYSIDE.

THE COASTLINE

Northern Ireland has an impressive coastline. There are many sandy beaches, rocky cliffs and extraordinary views.

The Giant's Causeway is the most famous area of the Northern Irish coastline because of the unusual rock formations.

NORTHERN IRELAND HAS 200 KILOMETRES OF COASTLINE.

THE REEFS AND SEA CAVES OF RATHLIN ISLAND ARE HOME TO SPONGES, CORALS, ANEMONES AND HYDROIDS, SOME OF WHICH ARE FOUND NOWHERE ELSE IN THE WORLD.

SEAWEED PICKED FROM THE COASTLINE OF NORTHERN IRELAND IS POPULAR AS A SOURCE OF VITAMINS AND MINERALS, AND AS AN INGREDIENT IN BEAUTY PRODUCTS.

TAKE A LOOK For information about wildlife around the Northern Irish coast, look at www.ulsterwildlife.org/living-seas

ROCK POOLS ALONG THE COAST OF NORTHERN IRELAND CAN CONTAIN ANEMONES AND STARFISH. INSHORE MUD PLAINS ARE FULL OF BRISTLE WORMS, SPIDER CRABS AND LOBSTERS.

The coastline of Northern Ireland is home to many different species of wildlife. Some parts of the coastline are popular with people who enjoy watersports.

15 SPECIES OF DOLPHINS, WHALES AND PORPOISES HAVE BEEN RECORDED ALONG THE COAST OF NORTHERN IRELAND.

THE LONG, GOLDEN BEACHES OF NORTHERN IRELAND ARE IDEAL FOR OUTDOOR SPORTS. SAILING, CANOEING, WALKING AND CLIMBING ARE ALSO POPULAR PASTIMES FOR VISITORS ALONG THE COAST.

PEOPLE

Northern Irish people are considered to be friendly, funny, and proud of their country. Some people in Northern Ireland consider themselves to be British. Others consider themselves to be Northern Irish.

The numbers of people from other cultures living in Northern Ireland increased by almost three-quarters between the **censuses** of 2001 and 2011.

IRISH (GAEILGE) WORDS

HELLO	DIA DUIT
BABY	LEANBH
BEAUTIFUL	ÁLAINN
LAKE	LOUGH
GOODBYE	SLÁN GO FÓILL
COLD	FUAR

SOME NORTHERN IRISH PEOPLE SPEAK IRISH, WHICH IS SOMETIMES CALLED GAEILGE.

THERE ARE MANY RURAL COMMUNITIES ACROSS NORTHERN IRELAND.

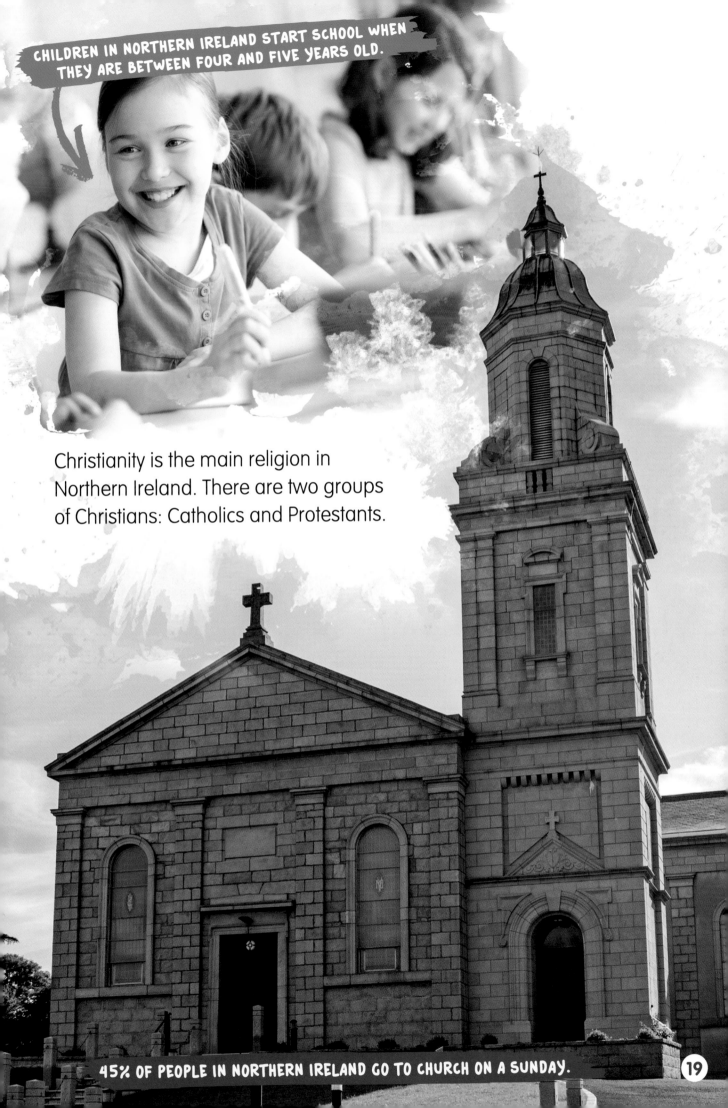

Christianity is the main religion in Northern Ireland. There are two groups of Christians: Catholics and Protestants.

CULTURE, LEISURE & TOURISM

In recent years, Northern Ireland has become a popular place for visitors from other countries. They come to see the breathtaking landscapes and to enjoy the culture and history of the country.

The capital city of Belfast is popular with tourists because of its busy shopping streets, museums, galleries and restaurants.

THE TITANIC VISITOR CENTRE IN BELFAST IS VISITED BY OVER 600,000 PEOPLE EVERY YEAR.

THE BOTANIC GARDENS IN BELFAST BACK ON TO THE CITY'S UNIVERSITY, AND ARE VISITED BY MANY TOURISTS EVERY YEAR.

CASTLEWELLAN FOREST PARK IS AT THE FOOT OF THE MOURNE MOUNTAINS AND IS FAMOUS FOR ITS PEACE MAZE AND ARBORETUM (A PLACE WHERE MANY DIFFERENT TYPES OF TREES ARE GROWN) WHICH WAS STARTED IN 1740.

There are also many smaller towns and villages that are full of interesting history. Many have inspired famous writers, artists and musicians.

CARRICKFERGUS CASTLE IN COUNTY ANTRIM IS JUST ONE OF THE MANY PLACES IN NORTHERN IRELAND THAT HAS BEEN USED FOR FILM LOCATIONS IN THE PAST. IT ATTRACTS MANY TOURISTS.

SPORT

Sport plays an important part in the culture of Northern Ireland, and many people play sports as well as being supporters.

Sports such as football, rugby, cricket and golf are all popular in Northern Ireland as well as a number of traditional sports such as Gaelic football, Gaelic handball, Camogie and Hurling.

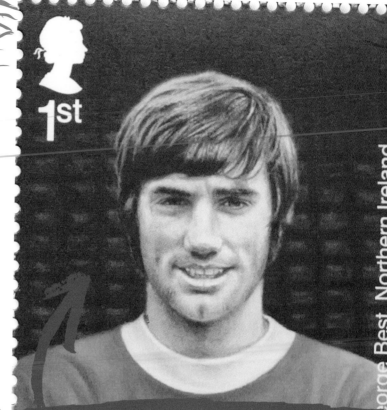

1st

George Best, Northern Ireland

GEORGE BEST, WHO WAS CONSIDERED TO BE ONE OF THE MOST TALENTED FOOTBALLERS IN THE WORLD, WAS BORN IN BELFAST IN 1946. HE PLAYED FOR MANCHESTER UNITED IN THE 1960s AND 1970s, AND FOR THE NATIONAL TEAM OF NORTHERN IRELAND.

HURLING IS A FAST GAME PLAYED WITH A STICK AND A HARD BALL. PLAYERS WEAR HELMETS AND SHIN PADS TO PROTECT THEMSELVES.

NORTHERN IRISH RUGBY PLAYERS PLAY AT INTERNATIONAL LEVEL FOR A TEAM THAT IS MADE UP OF PLAYERS FROM THE WHOLE OF IRELAND. THEY PLAY TOGETHER IN TOURNAMENTS SUCH AS THE RUGBY WORLD CUP AND THE SIX NATIONS CHAMPIONSHIPS.

There are many golf courses in Northern Ireland, and this makes it a popular place for golfers from all over the world, as well as for international competitions.

RORY McILROY IS ONE OF THE WORLD'S MOST SUCCESSFUL GOLFERS. HE WAS BORN IN COUNTY DOWN.

TRADITIONS

Northern Ireland is a country full of traditions and national pride. The people there enjoy many <u>festivals</u> and events throughout the year that celebrate their culture, customs and history.

Traditions such as Irish dancing and celebrating St Patrick's Day are shared with the whole of Ireland, and with Irish people who live in other countries around the world.

IRISH DANCING HAS BECOME FAMOUS AND POPULAR ACROSS THE WORLD. IRISH DANCE COMPETITIONS ARE CALLED FEISEANNA. THE DANCERS ARE JUDGED ON STYLE, GRACE AND RHYTHM.

THERE ARE NO SNAKES IN IRELAND. AN OLD STORY SAYS THAT ST PATRICK CHASED THEM ALL INTO THE SEA.

TRADITIONAL MUSIC IS POPULAR IN NORTHERN IRELAND. A TRADITIONAL MUSIC SESSION, CALLED A SEISÚN, OFTEN INCLUDES GUITARS, FIDDLES, BANJOS, FLUTES AND TRADITIONAL DRUMS CALLED BODHARN.

TAKE A LOOK For more information about customs and traditions in Ireland, visit **www.irishcultureandcustoms.com**

BOXTY IS A TRADITIONAL DISH ACROSS IRELAND. IT IS BELIEVED THAT THE RECIPE FIRST APPEARED DURING THE POTATO FAMINE TO MAKE POTATOES FEED MORE PEOPLE.

Food and drink feature heavily in many Irish festivals. Favourites such as soda bread, boxty, and Irish whiskey are famous around the world.

THE SHAMROCK IS A TRADITIONAL SYMBOL OF IRELAND, AND IS OFTEN WORN ON CLOTHING BY PEOPLE CELEBRATING ST PATRICK'S DAY.

IRISH WHISKEY IS FAMOUS ACROSS THE WORLD, AND IS A TRADITIONAL DRINK FOR CELEBRATIONS IN THE WHOLE OF IRELAND. THE OLDEST WORKING DISTILLERY IN IRELAND IS BUSHMILLS DISTILLERY IN COUNTY ANTRIM, WHICH WAS OPENED IN 1608.

QUICK QUIZ

Have you been paying attention? Let's find out!
Take our quick quiz to see how much you have found out in this book.

1. WHAT IS THE CAPITAL CITY OF NORTHERN IRELAND?

2. HOW MANY PEOPLE VISIT THE TITANIC VISITOR CENTRE EACH YEAR?

3. HOW MANY COUNTIES ARE THERE IN NORTHERN IRELAND?

4. WHEN WAS THE OLD BELFAST CASTLE BUILT?

5. WHAT WAS THE NAME OF FINN McCOOL'S ENEMY?

6. HOW LONG IS THE MOURNE WALL?

7. HOW MANY SPECIES OF DOLPHINS, WHALES AND PORPOISES HAVE BEEN RECORDED ALONG THE COAST OF NORTHERN IRELAND?

8. WHAT IS THE NAME OF THE HIGHEST PEAK IN NORTHERN IRELAND?

9. HOW MANY KILOMETRES OF COASTLINE DOES NORTHERN IRELAND HAVE?

10. HOW OLD ARE CHILDREN IN NORTHERN IRELAND WHEN THEY START SCHOOL?

11. NAME TWO TYPES OF BIRD THAT CAN BE SEEN IN NORTHERN IRELAND.

12. WHAT IS THE MOST POPULAR VISITOR ATTRACTION IN NORTHERN IRELAND?

13. WHERE WAS RORY MCILROY BORN?

14. WHAT ARE IRISH DANCE COMPETITIONS CALLED?

15. WHAT DO SOME PEOPLE WEAR ON THEIR CLOTHES ON ST PATRICK'S DAY?

16. WHAT DID ST PATRICK SUPPOSEDLY CHASE INTO THE SEA?

17. WHAT IS A TRADITIONAL MUSIC SESSION CALLED IN NORTHERN IRELAND?

18. WHAT IS BOXTY?

19. WHICH FOOTBALL TEAMS DID GEORGE BEST PLAY FOR?

20. HOW MANY SQUARE KM OF PARKLAND DOES BELFAST CONTAIN?

USEFUL LINKS

**Useful websites to help you find out
more about Northern Ireland**

WWW.ASKABOUTIRELAND.IE

WWW.DISCOVERNORTHERNIRELAND.COM

WWW.LONELYPLANET.COM/IRELAND/NORTHERN-IRELAND

WWW.BBC.CO.UK/NORTHERNIRELAND/LANDSCAPES

WWW.ULSTERWILDLIFE.ORG/LIVING-LANDSCAPES

WWW.ULSTERWILDLIFE.ORG/LIVING-SEAS

WWW.CULTURENORTHERNIRELAND.ORG

WWW.IRISHCULTUREANDCUSTOMS.COM

PLACES TO VISIT

Interesting places to visit in Northern Ireland

TITANIC BELFAST
www.titanicbelfast.com

PARLIAMENT BUILDINGS, STORMONT, BELFAST
www.niassembly.gov.uk/visit-and-learning/stormont-estate

THE MOURNE MOUNTAINS
www.ireland.com/what-is-available/walking-and-hiking/mountain-and-hill-walks/articles/mourne-mountains/

THE GIANT'S CAUSEWAY
www.nationaltrust.org.uk/giants-causeway

ARMAGH COUNTY MUSEUM
www.nmni.com/home.aspx

RATHLIN ISLAND
www.rathlin-island.co.uk

W5 INTERACTIVE DISCOVERY CENTRE
www.w5online.co.uk

CARRICKFERGUS CASTLE
www.discovernorthernireland.com/carrickfergus-castle-carrickfergus-p2814

GLOSSARY

BC	'before Christ', it is used to mark dates that occurred before the starting year of most calendars
CENSUSES	official counts of all the people who live in the country
CLIMATE	weather conditions
CONFLICT	active disagreement between people, often violent
CULTURE	the way of life and traditions of a group of people
CURRENCY	the money a country uses
DEPICTING	showing something in pictures
DIAMETER	the distance through the centre of an object
FESTIVALS	occasions where people celebrate and enjoy culture
LANDMARKS	places or buildings that are easily recognised
LANDSCAPE	physical features such as mountains, rivers, hills or coastlines
LOUGH	a lake
PARTITION	the time when six counties in the north of Ireland became a separate country to the rest of Ireland
POLITICAL MURALS	artwork painted on walls to show thoughts and feelings about The Troubles
RESEARCH FACILITY	a building that is built to learn and find out about things
THE TROUBLES	a period of time from 1969–1997 when British politicians, the British Army and different groups of people in Northern Ireland fought over what should happen to the country
TOURISTS	people who visit a place for pleasure

INDEX

Photo credits: Abbreviations: l-left, r-right, b-bottom, t-top, c-centre, m-middle, bg–background. Images are courtesy of Shutterstock.com. With thanks to Getty Images, Thinkstock Photo and iStockphoto. Front Cover – tr – Daz Stock. mr, bl – Josemaria Toscano. tl – Aitormmfoto. 3tr – Diego Barbieri. 3b –Ryan Simpson. 4 – okili77. 4bl – tanatat. 5tl – MiaQu. 5ml – Horia Bogdan. 5mr – Serg Zastavkin. 5r – Gabriela Insuratelu. 5bl –Aitormmfoto. 5br – Mike Flippo. 6tr – Robert Zp. 6bc – trevorb. 7tr – Josemaria Toscano. 7tl – Joseph Sohm. 7bc – stenic56. 8tr, 10tr, 16tr – PHB.cz (Richard Semik). 8ml – Josemaria Toscano . 8bc – sebafolla. 9tc – stenic56. 9mr – Stephen Lavery. 9bc – Gigi Peis. 10bc – eAlisa. 11tc – aleramo. 11bc – Jane McIlroy. 12bc, 19bc – stenic56. 12tr – Boris15. 13bc, 13tc – Spumador. 14tr – Netta07. 14bc – Dasha Kolesnikova. 15bl – Volodymyr Burdiak. 15tc – Peter Schwarz. 15br – Bildagentur Zoonar GmbH. 16bc – RUZvOLD. 17 – Cary Kalscheuer. 17mr – Ricardo Canino. 17bc – Semmick Photo. 18tr – Marcos Mesa Sam Wordley, Alexey Fedorenko. 18bc – rarena. 19tl – Pressmaster. 20tr, 21bc – SurangaSL. 20bc – Serg Zastavkin. 21tc – Martin Heaney. 22tr – catwalker. 22bc – Revel Pix LLC. 23tc – Paolo Bona. 23bc – David W. Leindecker. 24tr – DarkBird. 24bc – DarkBird. 25tc – Fanfo, vm2002. 25mr – Slavko Sereda. 25bc – Serg Zastavkin.